Adult Coloring Journal

Lined Note Pad and Anti Stress Coloring Patterns

V-Art Studio

Copyright © 2016 V-Art Studio

All rights reserved.

All rights reserved. No part of this publication may be reproduced, stored in retrieval system, copied in any form or by any means, electronic, mechanical, photocopying, recording or otherwise transmitted without written permission from the publisher. Please do not participate in or encourage piracy of this material in any way. You must not circulate this book in any format. V-Art Studio does not control or direct users' actions and is not responsible for the information or content shared, harm and/or actions of the book readers.

Don't Miss Another our Books.

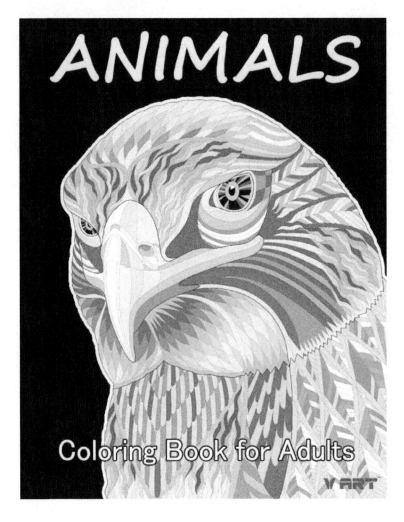

http://bit.ly/safari_coloring_b

ISBN : 9781523987931

(Use this ISBN for searching on amazon.com)

Join Us >> http://bit.ly/get_sample_free

When we release new book, we will send you the free sample first.

Printed in Great Britain
by Amazon